Fierce Jobs

Smokejump[ers]

by Julie Murray

Dash!
LEVELED READERS
An Imprint of Abdo Zoom • abdobooks.com

2

Dash!
LEVELED READERS

2

Level 1 – Beginning
Short and simple sentences with familiar words or patterns for children who are beginning to understand how letters and sounds go together.

Level 2 – Emerging
Longer words and sentences with more complex language patterns for readers who are practicing common words and letter sounds.

Level 3 – Transitional
More developed language and vocabulary for readers who are becoming more independent.

THIS BOOK CONTAINS RECYCLED MATERIALS

abdobooks.com

Published by Abdo Zoom, a division of ABDO, PO Box 398166, Minneapolis, Minnesota 55439. Copyright © 2021 by Abdo Consulting Group, Inc. International copyrights reserved in all countries. No part of this book may be reproduced in any form without written permission from the publisher. Dash!™ is a trademark and logo of Abdo Zoom.

Printed in the United States of America, North Mankato, Minnesota.
052020
092020

Photo Credits: Alamy, iStock, National Geographic Image Collection, newscom, Shutterstock, US Air Force
Production Contributors: Kenny Abdo, Jennie Forsberg, Grace Hansen, John Hansen
Design Contributors: Dorothy Toth, Neil Klinepier, Laura Graphenteen

Library of Congress Control Number: 2019956172

Publisher's Cataloging in Publication Data

Names: Murray, Julie, author.
Title: Smokejumpers / by Julie Murray
Description: Minneapolis, Minnesota : Abdo Zoom, 2021 | Series: Fierce jobs | Includes online resources and index.
Identifiers: ISBN 9781098221119 (lib. bdg.) | ISBN 9781644944066 (pbk.) |
    ISBN 9781098222093 (ebook) | ISBN 9781098222581 (Read-to-Me ebook)
Subjects: LCSH: Smokejumpers--Juvenile literature. | Fire fighters--Juvenile literature. | Wildfire fighters--Juvenile literature. | Hazardous occupations--Juvenile literature. | Occupations--Juvenile literature.
Classification: DDC 363.37--dc23

Table of Contents

Smokejumpers 4

Gear 10

More Facts 22

Glossary 23

Index 24

Online Resources 24

Smokejumpers

Smokejumpers are specially-trained firefighters. They don't ride on fire trucks. They jump out of airplanes!

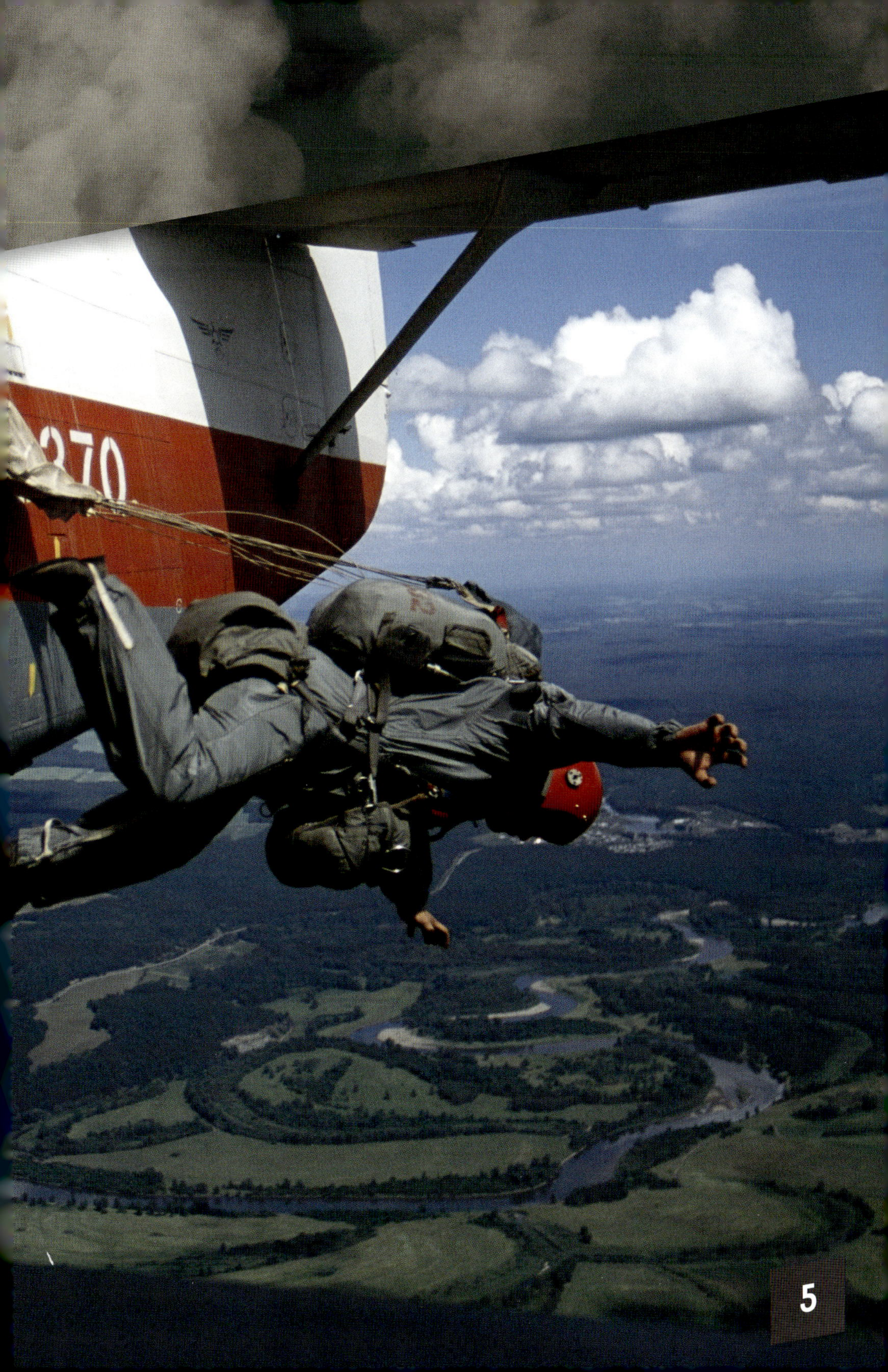

They usually work in **dense** forests or mountainous areas. These areas are hard to get to by vehicle.

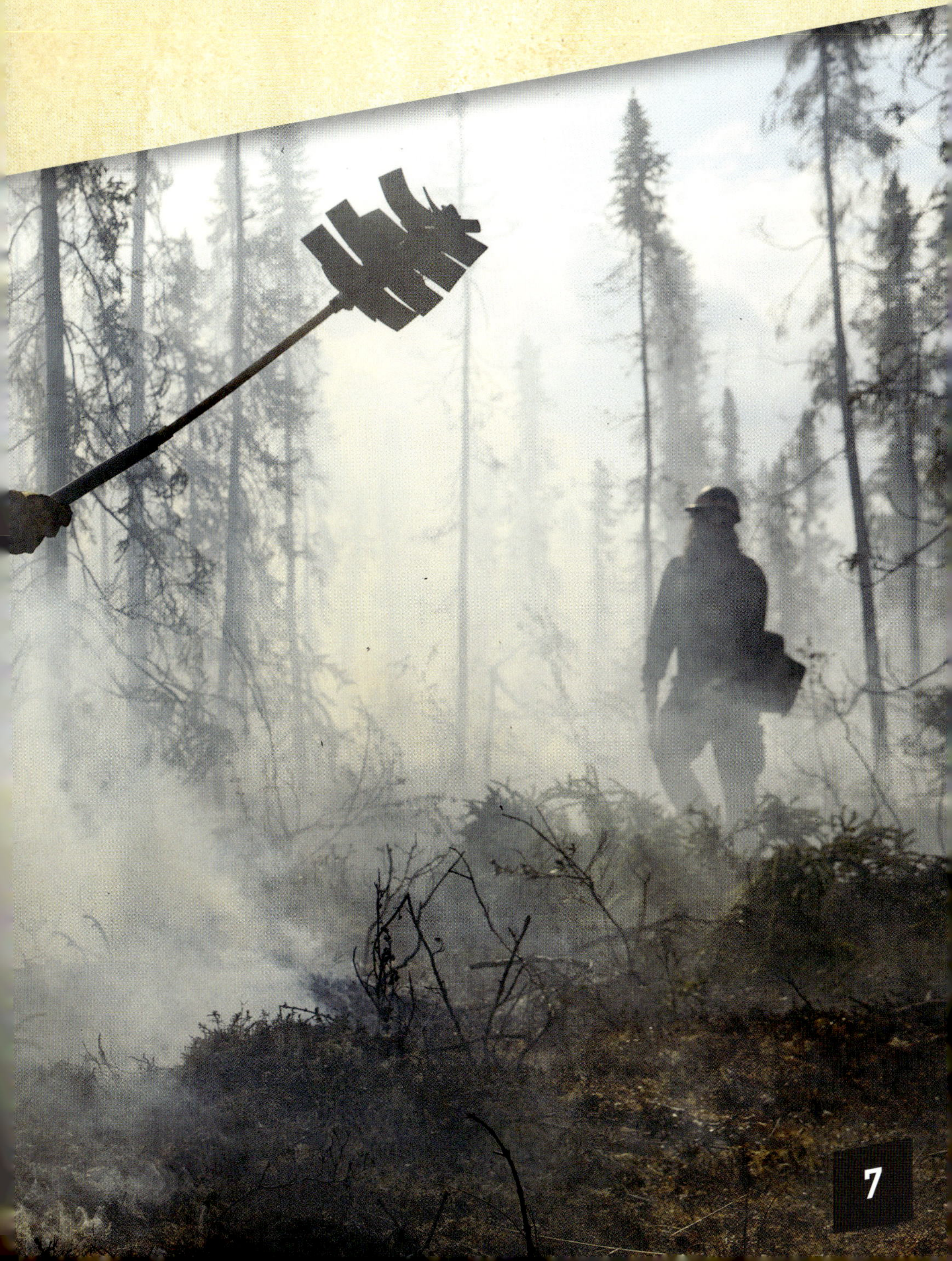

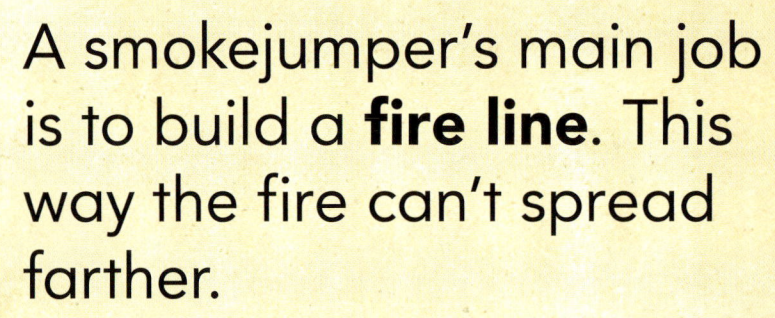

A smokejumper's main job is to build a **fire line**. This way the fire can't spread farther.

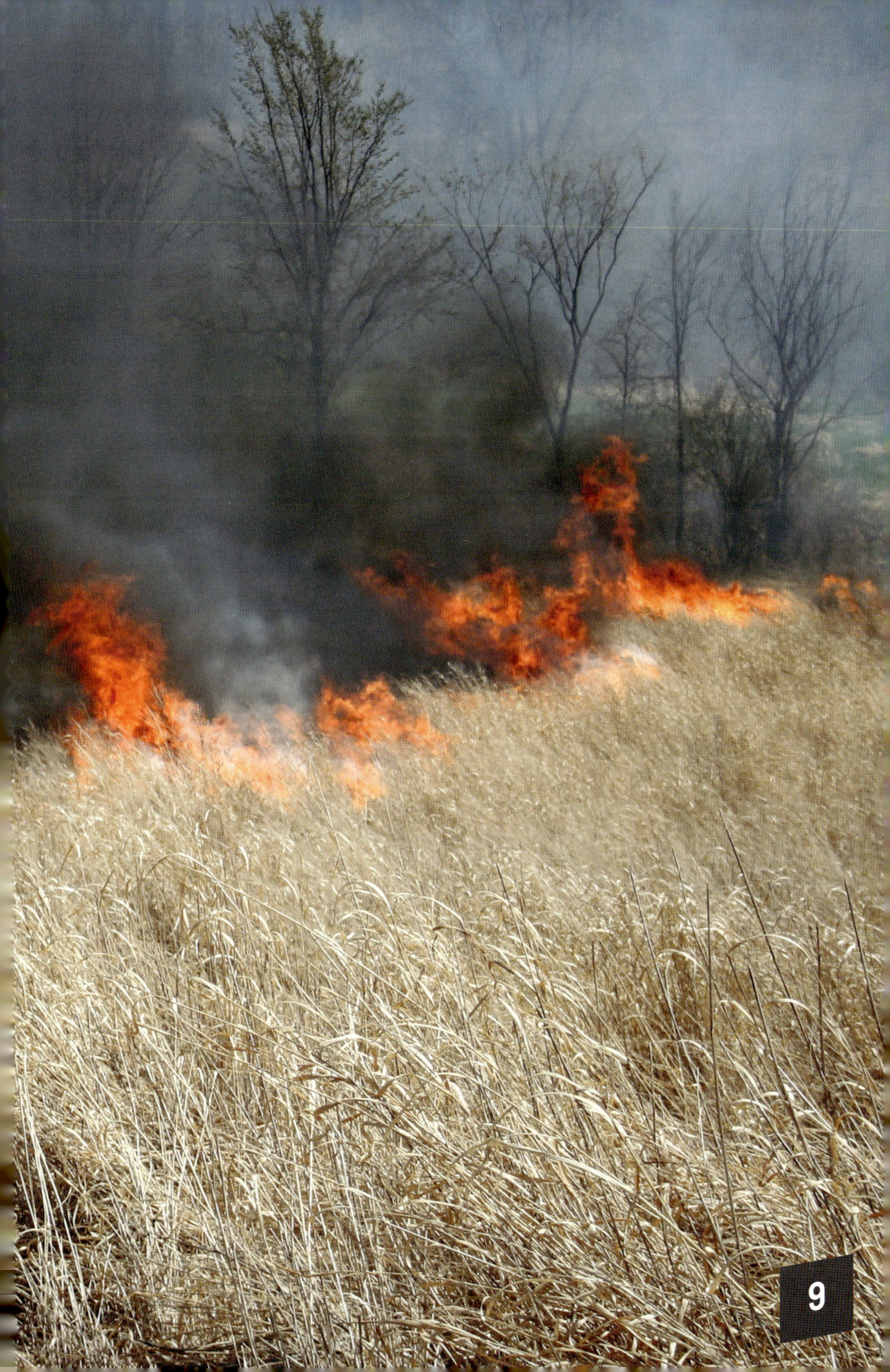

Gear

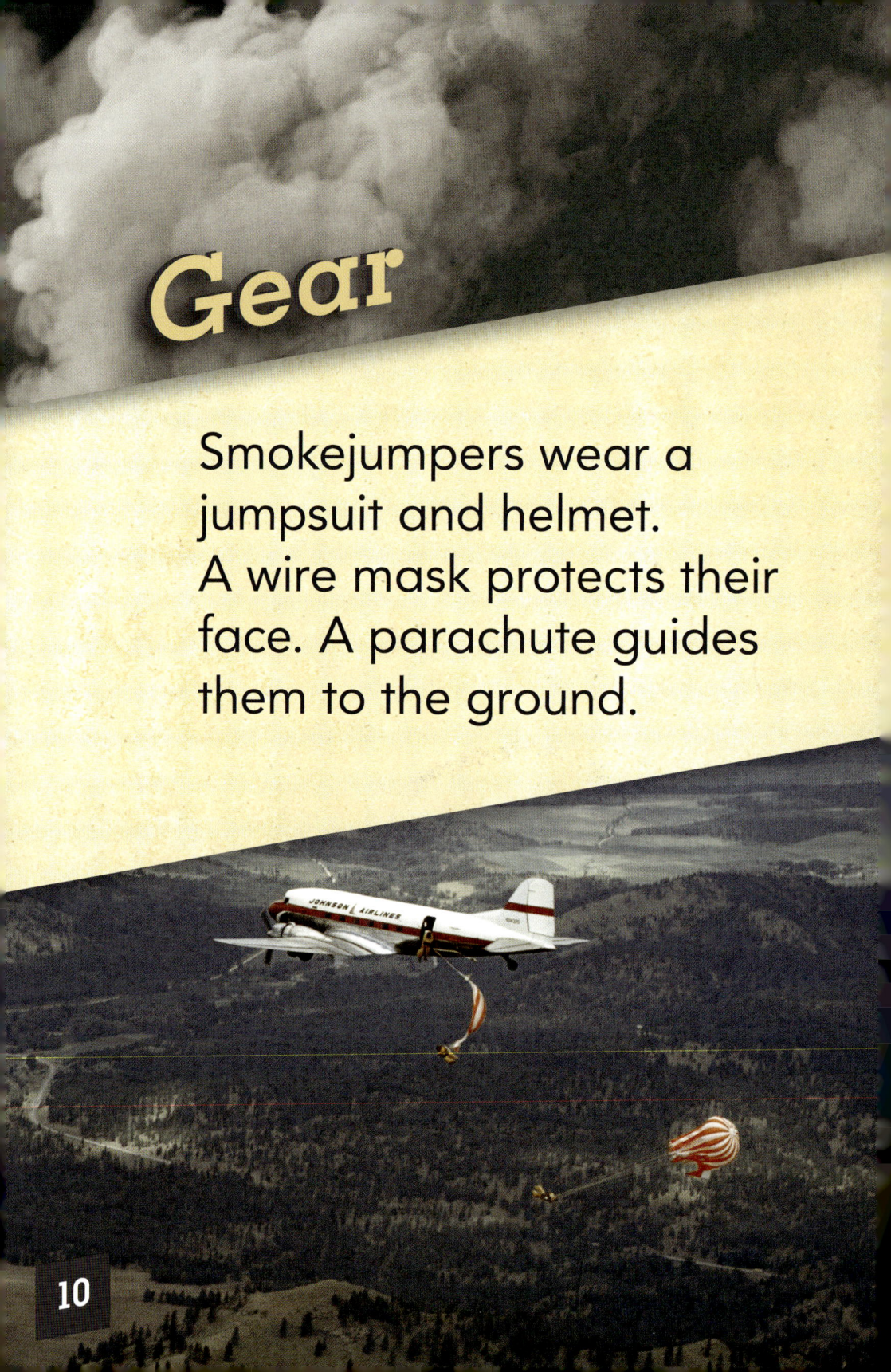

Smokejumpers wear a jumpsuit and helmet. A wire mask protects their face. A parachute guides them to the ground.

11

12

They wear special clothing under their jumpsuits. This clothing is fire-resistant. Smokejumpers carry a **two-way radio** with them.

14

Boxes of supplies land after the smokejumpers. These contain tools, food, and water.

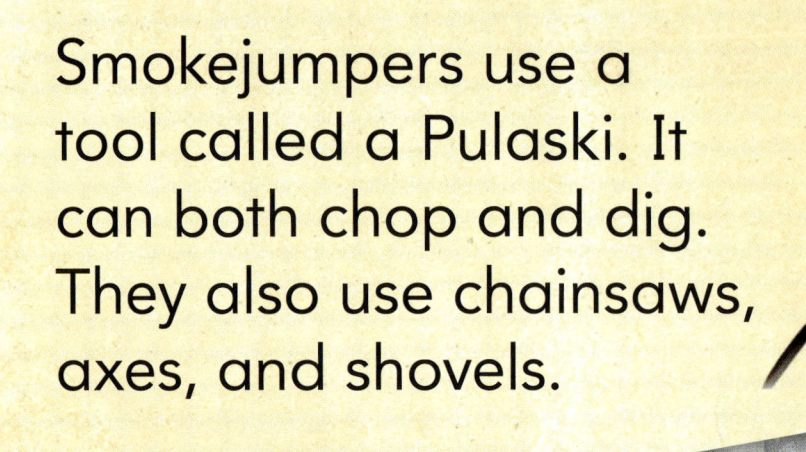

Smokejumpers use a tool called a Pulaski. It can both chop and dig. They also use chainsaws, axes, and shovels.

17

They also carry a **fire shelter**. Smokejumpers can get in this for protection. It is used if they get caught in the fire.

19

Smokejumpers risk their lives to do their job. They protect the land, animals, and people from fires every day.

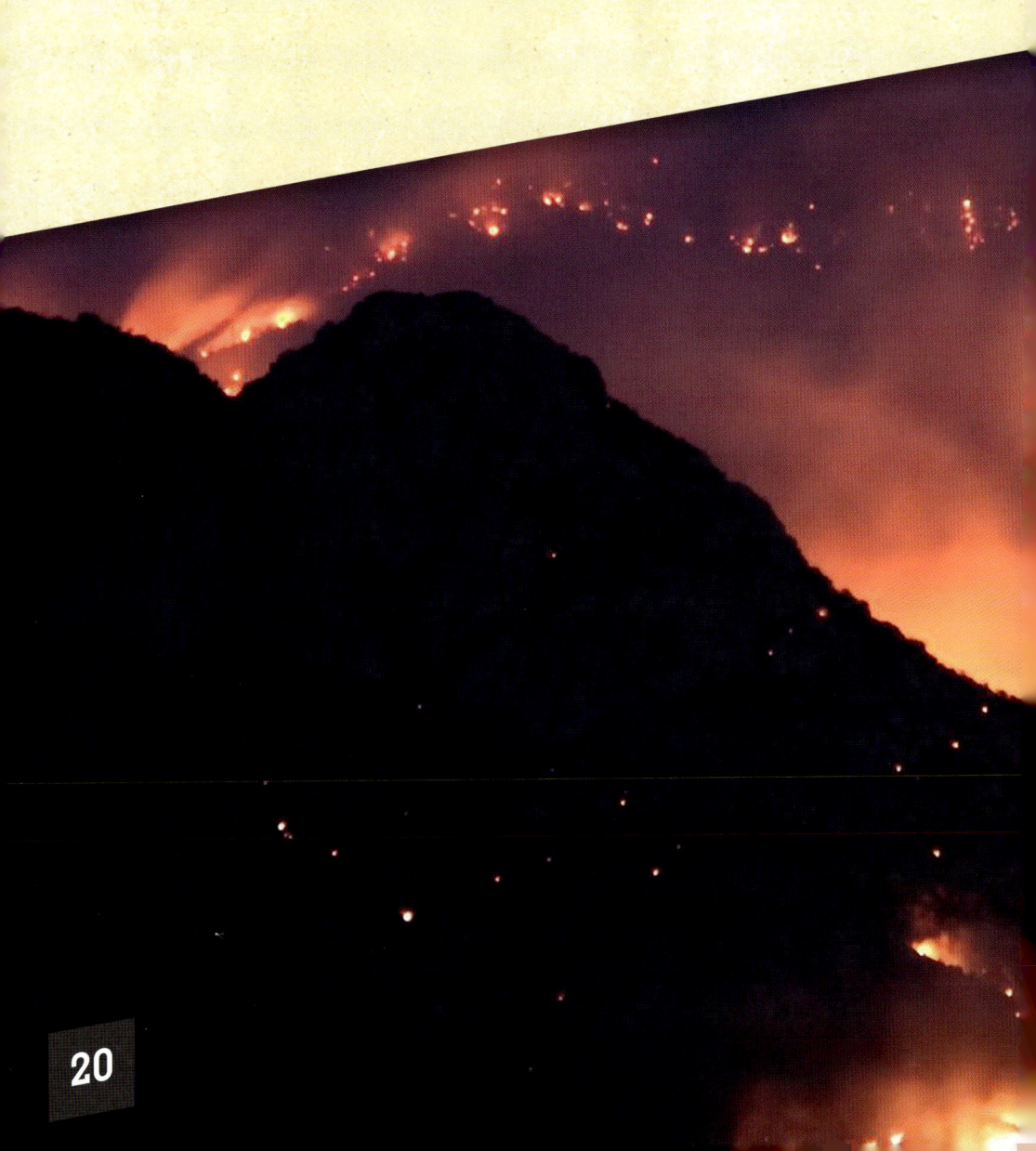

21

More Facts

- There are less than 500 smokejumpers in the US today.

- Smokejumpers mainly work during the dry season. This season lasts from spring until late fall.

- They must pass physical tests to get the job.

Glossary

dense – thick and hard to move through.

fire line – a strip of open land in a forest or prairie to stop the spread of a fire.

fire shelter – a safety device of last resort that is heat and fire resistant and is used by firefighters when trapped by wildfires.

two-way radio – a radio that can both transmit and receive radio waves for two-way communication.

Index

aircraft 4

firefighter 4

fire line 8

fire shelter 18

forests 6

gear 10, 13

mountains 6

parachute 10

safety 10, 13, 18

supplies 15

tools 15, 16

two-way radio 13

Online Resources

Booklinks
NONFICTION NETWORK
FREE! ONLINE NONFICTION RESOURCES

To learn more about smokejumpers, please visit **abdobooklinks.com** or scan this QR code. These links are routinely monitored and updated to provide the most current information available.